PANDA

PANDA

Written and Illustrated by
SUSAN BONNERS

A Young Yearling Book

Published by
Dell Publishing
a division of
The Bantam Doubleday Dell Publishing Group, Inc.
666 Fifth Avenue
New York, New York 10103

The trademark Yearling® is registered in the U.S.
Patent and Trademark Office.

ISBN: 0-440-40110-0

Reprinted by arrangement with Delacorte Press

Printed in the United States of America

October 1988

10 9 8 7 6 5 4 3

RAI

To Howard and Louanne,
who are good listeners

In a mountain forest of southwestern China,
a giant panda sits in a birch tree.

Snowflakes fall on her black and
white fur, but she does not look for shelter.

She has lived in snow
most of her life.

Early one autumn, she found
a den in a rocky mountainside.
There she made a nest out
of broken bamboo stalks.

While frosty winds blew through
the forest, she gave birth to her cub.

The cub was so tiny,
she could easily be covered
by one of her mother's paws.
    She weighed only five ounces.
    She was smaller than a kitten, but she had
a loud voice that sounded like a baby's cry.

The cub had just a thin covering of white fur.
Only her mother's warmth kept her alive.
Day and night, the mother
panda held her cub tightly
against her large, warm body.
She never put her down.

For several days, the mother panda stayed in the den and nursed her cub. Eventually, she had to eat.

Carefully, she looked outside.
She sniffed the chilly air. She listened
to the sounds of the forest.

Then, carrying her cub
in one paw, she left the den.

She did not have far to go for food.
Still cradling her cub, she ate some of
the bamboo that grew all around her.

Soon, the cub began to look like her mother.

By the time she was one month old,
she had a soft, thick coat
of black and white fur.

She could not crawl yet,
but she could roll around a little.

Now her mother could leave her
for a short time. Before she left,
the mother panda always put her in a hidden place.
At the cub's first cry, she hurried back
to soothe her by stroking her with a paw.

The cub grew quickly. At two months, she weighed
seven pounds, twenty times more than when she was born.
Her voice was softer now, a kind of bleating sound.
The mother panda played with her,
tossing her gently between her paws.

All this time, the cub's eyes
had been closed. She lived
in a world of sounds and smells.
She could hear her mother's
heart beating. She could
smell her and feel her warmth,
but she could not see her.

At two-and-a-half months,
her eyes opened,
and she began to see
the world around her.

She saw bamboo growing in tall thickets
that stayed green all winter.
There were spruce, birch,
and maple trees. Sometimes,
a golden monkey swung on the branches.

Birds flew overhead–
the titmouse, the nuthatch,
the laughing thrush.

At three months, she was able to crawl.
Now she could explore the world on her own.
Often, while her mother slept,
the cub sniffed over everything
she could find.

The cub did not spend all her time exploring.
Sometimes, she just played.

In the spring, the cub
was five months old and still
lived on her mother's milk.
She weighed twenty pounds.

One day, while her mother was eating
bamboo, the cub nibbled a leaf.

She crunched a thin shoot
with her milk teeth. As her jaws
became stronger, she ate
bigger and bigger stalks.
　　Her mother could eat woody stalks
an inch-and-a-half thick.

The mother liked to eat some leaves first.
Holding the stalk, she let herself
fall slowly backwards.

The mother panda ate
twenty pounds of bamboo every day.

Giant pandas have special linings
in their throats and stomachs to protect them.
They can even swallow splinters without being hurt.

Summer came. To escape the heat,
the cub and her mother went up to the cool
meadows above the forest.

In the meadows, they ate irises and
crocuses, vines and tufted grasses.

A panda has a special bone
in its wrist that works like a thumb,
so it can pick things up
with a very delicate grasp.

Now the cub was able to take care of herself,
but she stayed with her mother a while longer.
She kept growing and getting stronger.
When she was a year old, she weighed eighty pounds.

Her coat became wiry.
She lost her milk teeth
and grew large, permanent teeth.

Then, she went off to live on her own.

But she was not alone in the forest.
Little red pandas watched her
from their nests.
Pheasants flapped out of her way.

Takins tramped past her.
She learned to catch mice and birds
which she sometimes ate.

She was not afraid of any animals
but the snow leopard and the wild dog.

Honey from the beehive of a mountain farmer
was a special treat, but she could get it
only when no one was looking.

Her roly-poly walk was not very fast or graceful,
but with her short, powerful legs
she could go through the thickest forest.

The pads on her feet
were covered with hair,
giving her a good grip on the
steepest icy mountainside.
    She could even swim a
mountain stream if she had to.

She did most of her roaming
in twilight or darkness. She slept for a while
before dawn, and again in the afternoon
when the sun was high.

At the age of six, she was fully grown
and old enough to mate. She weighed 240 pounds
and was six feet long from nose to tail.

Male pandas are bigger. Fully grown,
they weigh about 300 pounds.

One spring day, she heard the bleat
of a male panda. He was following a trail of
scent marks she had left in the forest.

She made the marks by rubbing
a scent gland under her tail
against trees and rocks.

The male panda was also leaving
a trail of scent marks.
    Soon, the two pandas found each other
by following the marks.

On this day, both pandas were ready to mate. The female approached the male panda. He took her firmly in his front paws and they mated.

Then each panda went its own way again.
The female will have a cub of her own
in about five months. It will be born
in the autumn, just as she was.

She may live for another twenty years or more
and raise many cubs. Even so, giant pandas are rare.
They are found only in these mountains,
their wilderness home.